Relationship starts with RELATE!

*Person is used in this book to save time from writing "he/she, girlfriend/boyfriend, and husband/wife" all the time.

* I am aware that some of the language in this book caters to male/female relationships. This book was written with male/female relationships in mind. Before anyone starts bothering me about feeling left out or overlooked, I'm telling you now where my mind was at when I was writing this. If you want to write or read a relationship book of another kind, you're free to do so.*

* If you are a relationship counselor, expert, radio personality, author, motivational speaker, don't steal my style. I wrote this book because I never hear this kind of content being emphasized. I usually hear manipulative, confrontational, illogical, depressing and desperate advice. Sometimes I've heard some sensible things, but not enough. In my life I've heard and overheard too much advice that is bound to backfire. You're welcome to supplement your own style with aspects of my content, but don't steal my style. It's time for a new outlook on entering, being in and exiting relationships.*

*This book is the sum of my own thoughts, feelings, experiences and observations about relationships.

INTRODUCTION

I'm tired of hearing people whine and complain about relationships.

This book is FULL of things to think about, questions to get answers to, and some suggestions.

This is not an advice or self-help book because I'm not telling you what to do or how to do it. I'm just trying to direct your attention to some things. You can do whatever you think is best after that.

This book comes down to preventing suffering in relationships.
Everything in this book is to help you prevent suffering.

In no particular order:

THINGS TO THINK ABOUT

- A relationship should be an accomplishment, not an experiment!
  - By the time you get in a relationship, it should be because you know each other well enough to have confidence in it.
- Do things because of inspiration, not desperation.
  - Get involved with the person and interact with the person for good reasons and for the right reasons, not for bad reasons or for the wrong reasons.
- Cooperating vs. collaborating vs. competing
  - Competing within a relationship is unhealthy. Too many people are competing within relationships to see who can make who jealous, who can win fights, who can have the most replacements and substitutes on standby, who can hurt who's feelings, who can go the longest without acknowledging the other person, etc. Stop it.
  - Let the person collaborate with you, instead of expecting them to "cooperate" with you all the time. "Cooperate" isn't always as supportive of a word as it seems. Sometimes "cooperating" can mean just going along with something, even if you don't want to. There are times in life that we have to "cooperate" in that sense, but in relationships, people shouldn't feel like they have no choice but to go along with things. It's is a team effort. Interact with each other.
  - The idea of cooperation in a relationship is best used when you two are working on something together, and making decisions, not for when you want the person to submit and be who you want the person to be.
- When fighting, many couples make noise, but never make a point.

- Consider the shelf life of the relationship before you get in it.
  - Ask yourself, and each other, how long you think it will last. Discuss your thoughts.
- "My life doesn't revolve around you, it evolves around you."
  - People say "my life doesn't revolve around you" as a way to sting and stun their partner when they want some wiggle room or mental space. They're right. Life doesn't revolve around the other person, it evolves around the other person. Your life develops and synchronizes with the other person. So, if you don't want your life developing and synchronizing with the other person, don't be in that relationship.
- You should never feel outnumbered.
  - With the exception of fun and non-serious situations and conversations (such as games, hot topics, current events and harmless joking) you should never feel outnumbered. Your person should never side openly with everyone else in such a way that you feel helpless. Your significant other doesn't have to agree with you and what you think or how you feel, but you shouldn't feel like enemies in those situations either.
  - If you don't agree with your spouse or person in a group setting, reinforce your connection before you establish your independence on that subject. Ex: "I love you, but I don't feel the same about that subject." At least that way everyone in the room knows you still have rank!
  - Your significant other should never be defending someone to the point that you feel the other person is more important than you are.
- You should be able to express yourself without the other person taking it personal.

- If you can't be yourself, then the other person isn't dating YOU, they are dating who they want you to be. Also, if you're not able to be yourself, then you're not being fair to the other person because they don't get to experience the REAL you. If your friends and family get to experience the REAL you, then the person you're in love with should definitely get that experience!

- You should never have to perform, pretend, or be careful.
  - If you can't be yourself, then you can't be happy.
- Making an impression vs. making an impact...
  - The social definition of 'making an impact' is usually used to express that a person had a serious positive change on someone or something. We usually mean that this person has gotten your attention, kept your attention, and did something good with it, even if they didn't know it or weren't trying to. So, since an impression can be good or bad, concentrate more on if and how you two are impacting each other's lives.
- A relationship should be a J☺Y, not a jail.
- You should ENJ☺Y your relationship, not endure it.
  - You should be having fun, not fears. You should be celebrating your relationship, not tolerating it. You should be looking forward to it, not looking for a way out of it.
- DARE TO COMPARE!
  - Pay attention to how you treat strangers, hobbies, pets, friends, goals... and ask yourself how you treat your person compared to those things.
  - Do you take the time to find out how and why your person feels the way he/she feels?
  - Do you pay attention to your person's details the same way you pay attention to your "favorite things"?

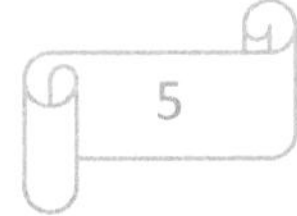

- Do you allow your person to vent like you allow other people to?
- Do you allow your person the freedom to express their moods like you allow other people to?
- Do you try as hard to understand your person's moods, thoughts and feelings as hard as you try to understand the things in life that are important to you?
- Do you talk to your person about himself/herself as much as you talk to your person about things you want them to listen to you talk about?

- Know your person as well as you know yourself.
  - Hint: This requires you to know yourself. The better you know yourself, the more curious and interested you'll be in knowing details about your partner.
  - Your person should know what they are getting involved in. The person should you're your personality, tolerance levels, temper, patience, what makes you mad, what you enJ☺Y, what you love & hate. Why want to be in a relationship with someone if you don't have a clue about any or all of those things? Why not find out what you're getting yourself in to?
  - That's real about any relationship. Why are people trying so hard to find out what they're getting themselves into when it comes to buying cars, dealing with contracts, signing up for credit cards, but not when they're dealing with people? Why are people concentrating so hard on what's on the menu and how their foods are prepared, but not studying the people that they are getting involved with?
- Some say fighting in relationships is unavoidable. I say it's unacceptable.
  - If you expect to fight, then you don't love the person. Do you EXPECT to fight you're your friends? (I'm laughing thinking

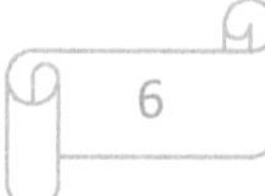

about fighting with my friends. This is actually the first time I've ever even had that thought).

- Brainstorm together about what to do if it ever feels like you're about to have a fight about something. Have a plan in place.
- Also, I laugh at people who are so polite to strangers and people in the community, but then they are mean and unfriendly to their boyfriend, girlfriend, husband, wife. That seems strange.

- Can you emotionally afford this person?
  - Before you get in a relationship with this person, evaluate on your own, and with the person, how hard or easy it's going to be to deal with the person's habits, style of communication, behavior, etc. It may or may not be worth it.
- I think it's always going to be natural for men and women to notice each other, even if involuntarily. The main thing is that if you're in a relationship, you shouldn't be seeking to look at other men and women on purpose. After all, you're in a relationship with the one who's best for you, aren't you?
- Your significant other may appreciate you asking and allowing them to vent, share, express and think out loud about other people.
  - Be serious. People might have crushes, attractions, unfinished business, leftover feelings, a handful of "what ifs?", etc. You'll be taken more seriously and treated more like a friend than a visitor in your person's life if you allow your significant other to do human things like talk, think out loud, brainstorm, and just have closure in general. Your (eventual) ability to have those kinds of talks will showcase how easily or poorly you'll be together as a couple.

- Remember, your person is going to have these talks regardless. If not with you, it will be with other friends, or with those other people who might be lingering and loitering in his/her mind.

- What are the possible side effects, if any, of this relationship on your health, feelings, safety, future, other relationships/friendships etc.
  - You should have an effect on each other, but not side effects.
- Panic vs. logic
  - Do things because they make sense, not because you're going crazy.
- PROVIDING vs. PROVING...
  - Too many people are trying to prove things to each other instead of trying to provide things to each other. You should be PROVIDING love, attention, etc. to each other. But instead, people are wasting time and energy trying to PROVE that they have options, trying to prove they love the person, trying to prove they are not cheating, trying to prove they are right for each other, etc.
  - Just provide the love, attention, quality time, attention to detail, etc. and you won't have to prove anything.
- Your person is not your pet or your puppet.
- Think about the effect of coincidentally claiming your exes.
  - "My ex-boyfriend. My ex-girlfriend. My ex-wife. My ex-husband."
  - Claiming your ex doesn't give you freedom from that time of your life. Even if you're simply referring to the person, you're still announcing a connection. You're still giving that person a title. It's just semantics really, but realize that saying "my" means that person is still YOURS!

- Some people are too busy trying to control the person instead of trying to concentrate on the person.
  - Just pay attention to the person. Imagine how we treat infants. We (are supposed to) support them, encourage them, listen to them, and take them seriously. We interrupt when they are about to hurt themselves or get in trouble. Other than that we let them think out loud, daydream, play, express themselves. But, why not to the ones we "love"?
- To some, sex is considered as an activity, something to do. To others it is a special event, reserved for special occasions, a special person.
  - Know what you're getting involved in before you get involved in it. That makes a difference in how everything goes after that.
- You should be with your natural match.
  - If you have to convince yourself that you are supposed to be with your person, you shouldn't be with the person.
- You should be filling in the blanks in each other's lives.
- Emotional probation
  - People are usually able to be themselves with their regular friends and be COMPLETELY comfortable because regular friends already know that they are going to be friends regardless.
  - However, I've noticed that with relationships people tend to tip toe constantly because of an unspoken emotional probation in which neither person wants to make a bad impression on the other person or lose the comfort level they've worked towards. With regular friends people usually relax, let their guard down and aren't worried about being

graded. People in relationships should have the luxury of that kind of guarantee like regular friends do.

- Regular friends EXPECT each other to be themselves. Regular friends put their personalities on display for each other! People in relationships should be able to enjoy the same freedom.

- It's more important to show love than to show off.
- Just because you're a fan of your person, doesn't mean you're an expert in your person. It takes time, attention, energy, patience, information, experiences, etc. to really be an expert in your person. Don't assume that you are as knowledgeable about your person as he/she is. Don't try to convince your person you know more about them than they do. If anything, try to convince them that you WANT to know as much about them as they know about themselves.
  - One day you will be an expert in your person. That should be your goal, not your assumption.
- Marriage should not only be a celebration of how much you love each other, but also a celebration of how READY you are for each other. It should be a celebration of how PREPARED you are for each other.
- What kind of friend are you if you disappear on your friend just because they suddenly have a relationship? I know about men and women who abandon or hide from their friends out of "respect" for the relationship. WHAT!?!?! What kind of friend is that?
  - I understand giving your friends some time to enjoy their relationship, but that's different from disappearing.

- Be thankful if your person tells you you're messing up.

- If your person tells you you're messing up, don't take it personally, take it seriously.

- Your person is joining your friends and family, but your friends and family are not joining your relationship.
- Does your culture interfere with your nature?
  - It's natural for men and women to be together. Some of the layers of life such as economic status, religion, racial taboos, etc. can prevent two people from living in love.
  - In my opinion, nature overrides culture.
  - It's none of my business, I'm just saying, what's more important? Nature, or culture?
  - Or, is your culture based on nature? Some say their culture is a format that mirrors the way nature intended it. If it is, then ok. If not, think about it.
  - There's many songs and movies about lovers who defied their culture for each other. Maybe those characters decided to obey their instincts instead of their instructions.
- Don't take advantage of each other, give each other the advantage!
- Your relationship should be valuable, not disposable.
- **LEVELS OF LOVE!**
  - **Too many "relationships" are only waist-love love.**
  - **Some relationships are heart-level love, in which people actually have feelings for each other and are enjoying getting to know each other.**
  - **Mind-level love is necessary. People are not only paying attention to each other, but actually studying each other.**
  - **Spirit-level love is ultimate.**
  - **Notice it goes from bottom to top, to a surrounding kind of love, a saturating kind of love.**
  - **It goes from obvious (waist level), to adventurous (heart level), to serious and curious (mind level), to JOYous and GLORIOUS (spirit level).**
  - **Hopefully relationships don't become tedious, devious or monotonous.**

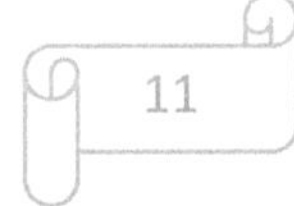

- Brainstorm on how to prevent potential and eventual problems so you can enjoy your relationship later.
  - If and when problems arise, you'll already know how the two of you want to handle them.
- If your person is complaining about an aspect of the relationship, it's an emergency, not background noise.
  - Even if the emergency is a false alarm, it's still an emergency until it's proven that it's not.
- You should be each other's priority, not each other's after thought.
- If your person is complaining about something, that person's feelings are more important than yours at that moment because that person brought it up. Have some manners and address their complaint.
- If/when problems arise, it's time to go in to action, **not time to go in to hiding!**
- Target practice...
  - Complaining should be for problem solving, not for target practice at the other person. If there is any target practice, it should be towards the problem, not the person.
  - It may feel like the person is using you for target practice, so panicking is understandable, but it may not be necessary.
  - If your person is aiming their complaints in your direction, realize that they may be aiming at the problem coming between you, or at a problem sneaking up behind you.
- Marriage is a different relationship status, not a different relationship.
  - Your marriage should be a CELEBRATION of your relationship, not an experiment based on how things are going so far.
  - Marriage is the finish line, not the race. Dating is the race.

- I was going to write a book called The War on Marriage. I was also going to write a book called Marriage Takes Courage. I'm not in the mood. As I said before, marriage is a different description,

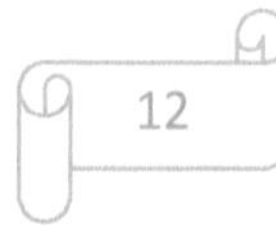

not a different relationship. It describes how great the dating was and that the two people are so satisfied with each other that they want to be together permanently. Dating compared to marriage is like comparing students and graduates. The "hard part" comes first, not last. Marriage is like graduating. It should be a relief.

- There's an often misused phrase "speaking it in to existence." I don't like the phrase. You don't talk anything in to existence. (According to the Bible, God did that. Everyone else usually has to take actions and a lot of follow up, in addition to whatever they apparently "spoke in to existence.") Anyway, for the sake of this entry, people are speaking "work-like" marriages in to existence.
- I always hear "marriage takes work. It's going to be work", etc. etc.
- I think people tend to say this out of expectation, more so than from experience. After all, experiences and expectations affect each other.
- So people speak work-like marriage in to existence, take a labor-like approach, and the result is that they create an atmosphere of struggle and stress.

- In a marriage, you are each other's priority. Your children, if you have any, are both of your responsibility, but you are still each other's priority. You still have to have a wonderful marriage long after the children move on to their own relationships in life.
- There's no privacy in a marriage, no secrecy.
- A lot of relationship advice concentrates on sex as a solution to relationship issues. Sex is not a solution, it is an action, and in many cases it is a distraction. Even animals have sex. It's a basic behavior in life. Our lives are more complex than animals and therefore it is necessary to solve issues at the mind-level, not just the waist level or heart level. "Facts before feelings" is a favorite phrase I use. Facts start from the mind, feelings are in the heart level, then on down. Trying to solve fact-related issues, mind-level issues, from the waist level is useless.

  - If two people's sex life is the issue in their relationship it is my opinion that those people can and should figure that out together.
- Your spouse is not your tag-a-long with limited access to you or your life. Your spouse is your love-twin.
- In sports, one goal is to keep the same team and keep winning. Athletes and sports organizations want to establish winning teams and have a dynasty in which they keep winning for a long time. They want to get comfortable and have a series of successes. They are proud of themselves for winning with whom they have.
  - In relationships, we celebrate dynasties such as long marriages, but the world is more excited about sports dynasties than relationship dynasties.
- Productive communication is the most effective.
  - Get your point across in a productive way.
  - Obviously there might be a mixture of facts and feelings when sharing your message, but get it out.
  - All feelings, the best and the worst, need to be shared. You have to get them out in order to be comfortable.
  - Even cursing someone out is technically communication, but it's not productive or comfortable communication. The person getting cussed out will probably get distracted by all of those junk words in your message. Find the best way to make your point without sticking yourself with it.
- Customer service from businesses tends to be better than the service people in relationships tend to provide to each other. That doesn't make sense. Business interactions are momentary. Relationship interactions are ongoing.
- You should be LIVELY in your relationship, not nervous.

- People don't usually see their regular friends as disposable, they are considered valuable. People usually make sure their friendships are in good condition. People seem to value their friends as though they **BELONG** in their lives. However, people in relationships often treat their person as if they are disposable and can be replaced. It's true, a relationship partner can be replaced, but if the person is so disposable and replaceable, why be in a *relationship* with that person in the first place? That's a waste of *both* people's time.
- Be with the person who **BELONGS** in your life and whose life you **BELONG** in.
- I used to joke and say "men are like trees, women are like the wind." Men have to be rooted. We may lose some leaves, stems and branches when the howling winds of womanhood start up, we may even lose a limb, but we have to still be standing when it's all over…
- Love at first sight is not the only way to know you've met the right person.
    - If you're lucky it can happen that way. You'll make eye contact, have a meeting in your minds and agree without words that you belong together. But for everyone else, it takes some double checking.
- You deserve a low maintenance relationship even if your person is high maintenance.
    - You should know if your person is high maintenance, fussy, messy, emotional, if the person overreacts, is nonchalant, doesn't take anything seriously, can't manage money, has a temper, etc. YOU SHOULD KNOW ALL OF THAT **BEFORE** YOU GET IN A RELATIONSHIP WITH THE PERSON! However, regardless of the person's habits and details, if you still want

to be in a relationship with that kind of person anyway, you'll already be ready for all of those things. Even if the person is a handful of headaches to you, you should already know how to deal with it before you get in the relationship.

- Costume jewelry on ring finger...
  - A good man is not going to flirt, recruit or devote himself to a woman with a ring on. I know single women wear rings on their ring finger to keep the wrong men away. I know single women do it to make themselves look and feel like they have a husband or fiancé. But, a good man is not going to even pay attention to you once he sees you're in a ringed-relationship. In the meantime, that man who might be meant for you, will be off looking for a naked finger.
- "It wasn't meant to be"
  - Maybe it was. Maybe it was meant to be and YOU messed it up.
  - But, if it wasn't meant to be with a particular person, move on. Your person is waiting for you! You should be looking for each other. Think of this world as one big game of hide-and-seek. Not that you two are intentionally hiding from each other, but rather that you are sometimes you're hidden in your jobs, hobbies, daily lives. Just ENJ☺Y the fun and suspense of trying to locate each other in this earth-sized playground.
- Are you in each other's way?
  - People usually keep friendships with people who are not in their way socially, academically, financially, emotionally, etc. So, why then do people stay in relationships with people who are in their way? I don't know. That's an entirely separate book (of mine called "Choices & Chances"), but the simple answer is that they shouldn't do it.

- Are you a couple, or just a couple of people?
- The problem with being wrong in a relationship is that sometimes the other person uses it as a chance to be mean to the other person and establish some sort of rank, even if for the moment. Compare that to how regular friends usually rub in the fact that one of them was right. Usually, regular friends brag in a playful, harmless or helpful manner.
- RANK-
  - There shouldn't be any rank in a relationship. Maybe there should be some defined or fluid leadership, maybe there should be some agreed upon or unspoken roles, but with rank comes superiority and inferiority. Along with rank, within a relationship, comes resentment and an instinct to overcome. It stops being fun.
  - I can imagine crews of regular friends in which someone is seen as the leader of the group, but even if that person has rank, there's still a common bond that makes everyone equal in a way. The rank is granted to that friend and everyone is comfortable with it. The rank in a friendship group serves its purpose for cohesion and inspiration.
  - Rank within a relationship makes one person more important than the other.
- Company vs. companion
  - Are you just keeping each other company, or are you companions?
  - Company is temporary, short term, or just filling a role (as far as dating is concerned).
  - Companion is long term, someone you are compatible with.
- Customize vs. Realize

- Don't try to customize the person, just try to realize who the person is, and then figure out if you can be happy with that (kind of) person.
- The planet is FULL of people. Don't panic if the couple of people you've encountered in life aren't "the 1".

• Everyone is usually on their best behavior until you get to know them.
  - Never rely on how people present themselves, depend on how people behave themselves over time. ***IT MAY TAKE A WHILE*** to see how people treat you during all of their different moods, how seriously they take life, themselves, you, how responsible they are, how consistent they are, how mature they are, etc.
  - By the way, maturity has nothing to do with behavior and everything to do with responsibility. Just because a person is playful, silly, still enjoys some of the same things from their childhood or doesn't take everything as seriously as you do, DOES NOT mean that the person is immature. Immature, according to me, has more to do with people who are not keeping up with the things that are considered responsible for the stage of life they are in.

• People seem to separate themselves from everything unsatisfactory, except for other people.
  - We spit out bad food, we quit jobs, we take off painful or "ugly" shoes and clothes. We avoid bad smelling air, but it takes too long for some people to separate from unsatisfactory people. I don't know why. People can do way more harm to you emotionally, mentally, physically, spiritually. People can really make you suffer. You may regret tasting bad food or wearing something you should have

thought twice about, but not as much as you'll regret wasting time with the wrong person.

- Compatibility vs. availability
  - Too many people are, or were, in relationships simply because the other person is/was available. Availability does not guarantee compatibility. Do what it takes to find out if you're compatible. Take the time, have the talks, take your notes on the person, study the person, observe the person, wait for consistency in the person's behavior and evaluate your own thoughts and feelings through it all.
  - Growing up, I've heard a lot of Christian people advocate diving in to a marriage or relationship with another Christian just because the other person is a Christian and somehow they think that will guarantee a successful relationship. If that was the case, you could pair up every two single Christians RIGHT NOW and have instant successful marriages! There wouldn't need to be any 'singles ministries', marriage ministries, marriage counselling, or divorces. I'm not making this about Christians, it's just the first thing that came to mind as an example of how availability doesn't guarantee compatibility.
- Don't skip steps.
  - Some people are lucky enough for everything to happen real fast and to go really well. GOOD for them. But, even people in those situations should be smart enough to make sure they're being thorough.
- Personal or natural schedules of affection and disclosure
  - Do things at the right times for the right reasons.
  - Do things when it makes sense to do them
  - Discuss things when the time is right. (Hint, the time is right when they cross your mind, or not too long afterwards)

- Some people see you as an accessory, some see you as a necessity.
  - Which one are you in your relationship?
  - Are you a tag-a-long or do you be-long?
- Peer pressure
  - Don't make relationship errors due to peer pressure. Do things that make sense.
- Excuse yourself from the relationship if/when it's necessary.
- Unanimous and Anonymous
  - Only a unanimous decision can create and continue a relationship.
  - If/when it is necessary to excuse yourself from your relationship, express that and demonstrate that. Regardless of the other person's insistence that you will remain a relationship member, that person's words are useless. Become anonymous if you have to.
- Does the person want you because you are somebody, or just for some of your body?
  - This is a common complaint. It happens to men and women, but it's usually women expressing how they feel they are or were being used for sexual actions. So, back to the question. Get your answer.
- Difference between fans and cheerleader…
  - I used to say I wanted a cheerleader to be there for me during this "game of life", but also that I had to win this game of life with or without her. I always said eventually I'd hear her cheering for me. There's a difference between fans and cheerleaders. You still have to try to win the game of life until your cheerleader shows up, but her presence can be a game changer.

- You should know they are "that kind" of person BEFORE you agree to be in a relationship.
    - (I already wrote something like this, but I want to include it here again)
- *If your relationship was money:*
    - *Earn your relationship, put it in a savings account and leave it alone. Put your feelings in a checking account and spend them as necessary. Put your energy on standby like pocket money/petty cash and enjoy it.*
    - Ironically, I always say "finance has nothing to do with romance". Finance may have something to do with how much you're able to concentrate on each other at times, but it should never have anything to do with how you feel about each other. Financial issues are obvious distractions, even for single people dealing with their own finances, but money should never affect your feelings like that. If it does, your relationship will never be stable, your mood will always be at the mercy of your money.
- Bragging rights
    - Ideally, no one would be able to brag and say they've been with your person, that they have had the one of a kind experience that you are having or that you are looking forward to having. If you've dated before, had sex before, been married before, any of the "befores", you owe each other to make sure that no one else can brag from now on.
    - Outsiders are not equal to your person, so they should not have equal experiences, access, or special attention that you give/get.
- GIVE IT TO YOUR FAVORITE!

- If you're out having sex with a bunch of people, what do you think your future wife/husband will be doing in the meantime? Maybe your future spouse will be out having sex with a bunch of other people too. Maybe your future spouse will be patiently waiting to meet you. Maybe your future spouse will be suffering different kinds of emergencies in the meantime.
- The more time we waste with the wrong person, the less time we have to spend with the right person. While you're wasting time, having sex with, suffering with, partying with the wrong person, the right person (your future spouse) is just loitering in life, alone or with the wrong person, waiting to meet you.

My advice is FOR EVERYONE to get a life. Get a hobby, get a goal, "get some business" and concentrate. Even if it takes a while to meet the right person, **what you are doing in the meantime is becoming the person that he/she is looking forward to meeting.**

There's nothing wrong with meeting, greeting and dating people, but there's a time when you know it's the wrong person. Do yourself, that wrong person, and your future wife/husband a favor, by keeping it moving.

Don't waste time.

Hopefully you and the right person are looking for each other, not just looking forward to meeting each other.

SPEAKING OF WHICH…

- KEEP YOUR EYES OPEN.

- I think it's useless to follow the advice "don't look because you won't find the person". Why wouldn't you look for something/someone that you want in life? What I will say is don't get depressed or stressed trying to find the person. Get a life, live your life, and keep your eyes open. In other words, pay attention.
- Where will you meet your person? There should be an atmosphere of suspense because you never know where you two will meet.
- Pay attention, but pay yourself attention first. Get a life.

- Right person, right time, right reason™
    - Get in to a relationship with the right person at the right time for the right reason.
    - Otherwise, you'll be in a relationship with a decoy.
    - (This applies to all kinds of relationships, partnerships, memberships...)
- Marriage is a permanent date.
- Does the person deserve your (ongoing) time and attention?
- Is your relationship valuable or disposable?
    - I remember a saying from somewhere that said "You don't get with someone you want to be with, you get with someone who you can't be without."
    - Is the person you're with or considering, someone you can do without? There might be people you can consider being with for different reasons, but the real question is would it matter if you weren't with them?
- Your person should not get in your way, instead he or she should get in to your way of life.
    - That doesn't mean they have to be in to everything you're in to. It means they should fit in to your life instead of being in

your way. Having your person in your life should be a treat, not trouble.

- No suffering
  - There should be no suffering in your relationship. There may be some problem solving that needs to go on, but not suffering. You should be making each other's lives better, not worse.
- If you closed the doors on a relationship, be aware that the person you closed out may have, "spare keys." They may have a way of regaining your time and attention. You might have to "change the locks" on that door those emotional and mental doors that you closed so they can't reenter your life or your attention span in those ways whenever they feel like it.
  - Don't let an ex or a former person of interest have access to your future. That doesn't mean you have to ignore the person, pretend to be strangers or be unfriendly, but if you gave them the keys to your heart, your life, your mind, etc., you may have to update and upgrade your life in ways that the person doesn't fit in to anymore.
- Know your partner <u>as well as</u> you know yourself.
  - Hint: Requires you to know yourself.
- You should be interacting with each other, not interfering with each other.
- You should have an effect on each other, not cause side effects on each other.
- I think there's a difference between breaking up and not dating anymore.
  - Socially, "breaking up" usually gives the impression that something went wrong, something broke in the relationship. Some kind of bond or trust was broken.

  - It's possible that two people just lived out the life of the relationship and are still in good moods. I think it's ok for two people to say "We lived out our date-life" without being negative about it.
- Ask yourself why he/she deserves your time and attention.
- A relationship is like nourishment, it's not a punishment.
  - It's good for your soul, fills you up with feelings and keeps you happy and healthy.
  - If that description doesn't sound like your own relationship, study it more and start problem solving.
- You should be each other's hosts in your relationship, not each other's hostages.
- Be a gift to your person, don't use them as a gift to yourself.
- Join each other's lives without ruining each other's lives.
- Some people enjoy getting in the way of other people's relationships due to desperation or recreation. Watch out for them.
- Remember you are getting involved with a person AND their person-ality.
  - Many people deal with the person, the look, the idea of the person, the potential. But, what about the actual? What about who the person really is?
- Develop an alarm system for your relationship to keep trouble from intruding.
  - Don't wait until outsiders, doubt, fear, jealousy and so on have already gotten in to your relationship. Know your warning signs and what to keep an eye on so your relationship isn't infested with worst case scenarios.
- Evaluate your potential to suffer both with and without this person.

  - Don't just talk to yourself or your friends about it. Talk with the person about it. Explore all of the best and worst case scenarios and find out how you both feel about it all.
- Don't try to overcome the person, try to understand the person.
- Don't try to customize the person, just get accustomed to the person.
  - If you're trying to make the person in to what you want them to be, you don't like the person and shouldn't be with him/her.
  - Remember: There's a difference between having an effect on a person and having side effects.
  - You two will change each other's lives in different ways, and maybe even change each other a bit, but those things develop and happen naturally. If you're planning, plotting, scheming and scamming on how you can change the person, you're not being fair and you're not healthy for that person.
  - If that's not the right person for you, then you don't belong together, you both belong with someone else.
- A relationship should be an adventure, not torture!
- Be with someone who won't embarrass you.
- Be with someone who can keep your attention.
- Be with someone who makes love obvious and who makes it obvious they are serious about you.
- Be with someone who won't waste your time or attention.
- Your person is not your property, but rather your opportunity (to be happy).
- Remember you have a brain, not just a groin. Think about who you're with and why. It should be for reasons beyond sexual intentions.

  - Sex is a basic and obvious reason for men and women to be interested in each other.
  - Now, what else? What about the details of that person's life, lifestyle, behavior, etc…
- What are the possible side effects, if any, of this relationship (on your health, feelings, safety, future, other relationships/friendships etc.)
  - I may have written this already, but it's important.
- Do things before and during your relationship because of inspiration, not desperation.
- Do things before and during your relationship using logic, not panic.
  - Do what makes sense, not nonsense.
- Some people are too busy trying to control the other person instead of trying to concentrate on the person.
  - Just pay attention to the person. Imagine how we treat infants. We support them, encourage them, listen to them, we take them seriously. We interrupt when they are about to hurt themselves or get in trouble. Other than that we let them think out loud, daydream, express themselves, we study them and enjoy them. But why not to the ones we "love"?
- To some, sex is an activity, something to do. To others it is a special event reserved for special occasions, special people.
  - Know the difference and know which one applies to both of the people in the relationship.
- You should be able to ENJ☺Y your relationship, you shouldn't have to endure it.
- How much of a match are you two?
- Outsiders are not equal to the relationship members.

- Outsiders should not have the same experiences that the people in the relationship have. Outsiders shouldn't have the same access to each other's body's, time, etc....

- FAIRNESS AWARENESS!
  - Are you being more fair to other people than to your own person?
- EXPRESS, EXPLAIN, EXPLORE, EXAMINE and EXCHANGE
  - Do you express and explain yourself to your person as much as you express yourself to other people?
  - Do you actually explore feelings about yourself, life, your person, miscellaneous things with your person as much as you do with other people?
  - Do you examine each other's thoughts and feelings like you examine your change from a cashier, like you examine your food, like you examine yourself the moment you get hurt or cut?
  - Do you exchange enough, often enough?
- Attention span
  - Do you have as much of an attention span for your person as you do for everyone else and everything else?
- Do you want a sex life or sex habits?
  - My short answer to how to have the best possible sex with your person is to figure each other out.
  - You two people need to pay attention to each other and figure out what works best for YOU TWO. It's like dancing. You have to get used to being in each other's company.
  - If you depend on outside (re)sources, you will have sex habits instead of a sex life.
  - If you have had sex with someone else before and expect your person to do the sex habits of another person, or try to copy

things from a previous sex life, then you cannot have a sex life with your person. You can only have sex habits.

- On vs. ongoing
  - The phrase "it's on!" means it's ACTION TIME! It's true that for some relationships "it's on!', but that doesn't mean the relationship is ONgoing.
- If you like someone else or your person likes someone else, talk about it. You may realize:
  - The other person just reminds you of the person you're already with.
  - It's tempting, but it's not worth it.
  - You are uncomfortable with the same things about your relationship that your person is, which is why you might like someone else at that moment. Discuss those things and address those things.
  - You may realize your person has a point and that you two are not best for each other.
- Consistency
  - When the person shows you enough moods, attitudes, feelings, then you can make an emotionally careful move
- FACTS **BEFORE** FEELINGS!
  - It doesn't matter how you *feel* about the person, start and finish with the facts about the person: the facts about how you're treated, the facts about the potential for a successful relationship, the facts about if it makes sense to get in the relationship.
  - Your feelings don't change the facts, so respect the facts first.
- Make sure you're fair.
- Don't give to receive.

  - Don't give someone your time and attention because you want something back from them. Give them your time and attention simply because you want them to have it. THAT'S IT! THAT'S THE ONLY reason! If you end up getting a relationship out of it GREAT NEWS FOR Y☺U, but if you don't who cares? After all, that's not why you were being so nice in the first place, **IS IT?**
- Get in to a relationship when it makes sense to get in to one. Get in to a relationship with whom it MAKES SENSE to be in one with. (This applies to memberships, partnerships etc. as well.)
  - Some people want to be in relationships even if it doesn't make sense to be in a relationship. To these kind of people it doesn't matter if they're compatible or not, if they have good personalities or not, if anything. They just want to have someone. They just want to claim someone.
- I'm not one to doubt long distance relationships because 'RELATIONSHIP STARTS WITH RELATE'. It's all about how people relate to each other.
  - I always shut down the long distance relationships argument with the thought that there are people who live IN THE SAME HOME who can't get along, who can't relate to one another. Eventually the two people in the long distance relationship will be together, in the same place at the same time. It's a temporary distance, even if it's for a long time, it's still temporary.
  - - People don't have confidence in long distance relationships because they want access to the person for selfish (usually sexual or romantic) reasons, they don't trust the person, and they want more time to observe the person, experience the person and have a better chance of getting to know who they are getting involved with.

  - All of that is understandable, but just being in each other's company doesn't guarantee that you will have quality or productive interactions. You may just end up enjoying each other's company, but not paying enough attention to detail to know what's really going on. You may just end up being a supervisor over the person, rather than being a super companion.
- Be yourself. See who likes it and who doesn't.
- Contenders vs. pretenders
  - My buddy used to always say "Some people are pretenders, some are contenders".
  - If you're single, sort through the contenders and the pretenders.
- Find someone worth being with.
- Crash course!!!
  - No matter how long people take to get to know each other, you are still just getting a "CRASH COURSE". Unlike your friends and family, the person hasn't been around you enough to know you like your friends and family do. It's your responsibility to introduce them to any and everything they need to know about you. It's your job to give examples and experiences so being with you becomes 2nd nature to the person. Even if a person has known you for a long time, the person hasn't known you as a relationship partner. That's a different experience.
- Be the same person in the company of people that you are when you are alone.
- It could be better:
  - When people tell me it could be worse, my response is, "It could be better too."

- If there's tension between the two of you, either the tension is going to win, or the two of you are going to win. You decide.

- If you can't be your person's outlet, someone, or something else, will be.
  - Best case scenario, you will be an outlet.
  - Worst case scenario, the person will get another outlet or just leave you.
- Just because you know the person doesn't mean you know the personality.
  - (I know I wrote that earlier)
- Be careful with your person like you're careful with the food you're cooking
- When someone says "I'm in school (college) and this isn't a good time for me to be in a relationship", what they really mean is that they don't want to be distracted. BUT, a good relationship isn't going to be a distraction at all, it's going to be an addition to your life. A good partner is going to HELP you reach your potential, even if all they do is stay out of the way.
- If you are worried, nervous, skeptical, uncomfortable, etc. about your person having friends of the opposite sex, remember:
  - There's a difference between friends of the opposite sex and troublemakers/thrill- seekers of opposite sex.

- As I said in my song "JOYS & CONCERNS" on my album SPEAK UP , "Keep the peace, share the power, give the love"™!
  - Your person is the one you are going to have the most contact and interaction with. It might as well be peaceful. Who wants or needs ongoing turmoil with a person they see, talk to and think about so often?
  - Share the power. You don't have to be IN control as long as everything is UNDER control. Using a road trip example, you don't have to drive the entire distance, let the passenger drive some of the way.
  - Give the love.

- You shouldn't be guessing or assuming anything about your person.
- To avoid and prevent worst case scenarios, make sure you know what you're getting yourself involved in.
- Compromise vs. surrendering
  - There's a difference between compromising and surrendering.
  - Remember there's a few connotations to compromising. There's the kind of compromise in which people sacrifice a bit to get mutually satisfying results, and then there's the kind of compromise/surrendering where people disrespect themselves and have regrets.
- There's a difference between being curious about your person and being nosy
  - On one hand, it's better to be curious, just wondering things and approaching those things carefully and respectfully.
  - On the other hand, it's better to be nosy about some things, things that are not worth waiting to find out.
  - I think daters should be more curious than nosy.
  - I think spouses should be more nosey than curious.
  - Ultimately, everything should come out in the open so the people in a relationship can concentrate on each other, rather than being distracted by the things that are bothering them.
- Pretending vs. preparing for best and worst case scenarios…
  - I may have said this already, but it's better to prepare for worst case scenarios than to pretend they won't happen. In fact, preparing for them can help prevent them because you'll know what you're looking for.
  - Thinking out loud and brainstorming can expose people's intentions, problem solving styles, sense of responsibility, and how serious they (plan to) take the relationship.
- Later, Now or Never
  - When you realize that you're not sure if something is worth talking about, discussing, debating, arguing over, etc., ask each other if you're going to talk about it later, now or never.
  - Agree on whether or not it's worth the time and attention.

- Mentality, personality, reality
  - Know your person's mind, true self and how his/her life affects him/her.
- It's ok to feel sorry for the other person if they are going through things. Don't overlook their woes and just expect them to get back to their "duty" of being who you want them to be. That's not what their friends would do. Their friends would be helpful, inquisitive, sensitive, etc. You SHOULD BE friends with your person, and therefore it shouldn't be hard for you to be a friend when your person is in need.
- Smothering is not the worst thing in the world.
  - Think about it, someone thinks you're sooooo important that they want to be soooo dedicated to YOU.
  - Just express your comfort levels kindly
  - If the smothering is not your thing, then thank the person for the attention they give you and explain how it's not the best thing for you.
  - Get out of that relationship if you have to. Don't get in to it if you're not in it yet.
- Guilt trip
  - People don't usually give their friends the guilt trip to get what they want. If they do, it's usually in a harmless and momentary way in order to get them to share snacks, go see the movie they prefer or meaningless things like that.
  - Yet, many people in relationships tend to use the guilt trip as a means of controlling their relationship partner and making them uncomfortable.
- Inmates / persons in jail
  - Relationship starts with relate. Of course the daily interactions aren't possible like they are for free people, but if your person

is in jail suddenly or for a long time, the main thing is how you relate to each other.
- Do you relate better to any free person than you do to your inmate? If not, then the person in jail is still the person for you. You just have to get a life and be busy until the person is available again.
- If you can't wait, then the quality of your friendship will make that conversation easy. It will make sense because the inmate knows you well enough, and is a good enough friend to know that you are suffering. The inmate won't want you to wait for selfish reasons, the inmate will want you to reach your social potential.
- BUT, if you're just bored and want to have some company while the inmate is unavailable, think about getting a life and being busy.
- Just because your best friend is locked up doesn't mean you have to go get a new best friend in the meantime.

- Are you in your relationship for status or to make a statement?
  - You shouldn't be. You should be in your relationship because it's the best thing for both of you.
- Scare tactics in relationships are weird. Friends don't use scare tactics on each other.
- I'm not saying that you should only get in to relationships with a friend you already have. Obviously people meet strangers and get interested in each other. All I'm saying is that the people in relationships should have established a healthy friendship at some point before depending on each other as relationship partners.

- You should expect your person to enjoy you, not to obey you.
  - After all, you are FRIENDS, right?

  - People don't usually expect friends to be obedient
- Allow your person the courtesy of venting. It's got to come out somehow.
- If you can't enjoy talking freely and easily with your person like you do with your friends and family you're not in the right relationship or your relationship isn't a good quality one.

- Think out loud without getting loud.
- Your person is not your opponent, your person is a component of your life.
- Remember, unless you've known this person forever, you are playing catch up. You are not as familiar with this person as your friends and family are. So, either watch and learn, or take a crash course in this person's life, moods, attitudes, thought processes...
- "Don't think you're the only one who likes the same person you like!)
- If you're a person in a relationship who says "I never do anything right!", my only question is why not? When are you going to start?
  - If there is a problem, solve it.
  - Get results or get out of the relationship.
- If you are keeping score on who did what to who, who made who mad, who got on who's nerves, then you're concentrating on those things, when you should be concentrating on your person instead.
- If you're a person who was in a failed relationship and your reasoning is "It wasn't meant to be", I can't help but think that maybe it WAS meant to be. Maybe you messed it up.
  - Maybe the other person messed it up.
  - Some people like to default to "God has something better planned for you." How does that person know? Maybe God gave you the person he planned for you. Maybe someone just needs to accept the fact that they messed it up.

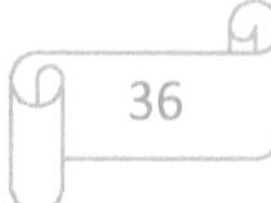

- In many situations I can imagine God saying "don't put my name in that. It's not MY fault."
- But, if it truly wasn't meant to be, then move on without leaving a trail of insults and excuses. Just keep going.

- The Golden Rule is N/A because who says everyone wants to be treated well?
  - "Treat them like you want to be treated" isn't a universal piece of advice. Some people like being mistreated or they tolerate more than they should.
  - I don't want to be treated like those kinds of people get treated.
  - Some people even EXPECT to be mistreated. It's a kind of normal that they are used to. They may not even be fully aware that the way they are being treated is unhealthy.
  - Treat people like they SHOULD be treated, not the way you want to be treated, just in case you don't care enough how you're treated. Just in case you don't have self-esteem.
- Attention span
  - It's not about getting each other's attention. It's about the attention SPAN. How long will you be able to keep each other's attention?
- People should be mentally compatible, even if not mentally identical.
- CHEATING:
  - Cheating is basically "trying to get away with something." Friends don't do that to each other. Friends may try to get the most out of their friendship with each other, but they don't try to get away with anything.

  - I think I said this already. But, friends don't try to get away with anything. A person who cheats is trying to get away with something. If you're friends, for real, with your person, you shouldn't be trying to get away with anything.

- At the moment you cheat, you tried to get away with something, therefore you are not a real friend. Therefore, you should not be in a relationship anymore because friendship is the foundation of relationships. Without a foundation, there's nothing for the relationship to rest on.
- In life, we don't want our friends to suffer. If someone wants you to cheat with them, what they are really saying is "I want your friend, who you're in a relationship with, to suffer." You know your relationship partner is going to be unhappy, etc., so why would you make your friend suffer? As people, we tend to take our friends' suffering very seriously. We don't tolerate the circumstances and we do everything we can to help them out of it. Those friends are classic kinds of friends. But here, I'm talking about your relationship partner, your spouse, etc.. If we can be so serious about our regular friends suffering, we should be way more serious about the idea or possibility of our relationship partners suffering. After all, you do have a friendship with your relationship person, don't you?
- Some people choose to work it out, think about it, talk about, promise honesty, etc. Either way, the relationship is being reset at that point. As the relationship is starting over, it is obviously not a relationship of two friends, it is a relationship with two members.
- Also, if you initiate the cheating, that means it was important to you, more important than your relationship. So, you shouldn't be in a relationship anymore since there's something more important than your relationship. If you allowed the outsider to have what he/she wanted from you, that means you think that person is more important than your friend who you are in a relationship with. So, you shouldn't be in the relationship anymore. You know your friend that you're

in a relationship with is going to be upset, so you are not a real friend. Again, you shouldn't be in the relationship.

- Why is sex so serious when it comes to cheating? Why is it so mean and meaningful for your person to have sex with someone else? Does it strike a primitive nerve, that maybe the outsider will introduce their own genes in to this life? Does it strike a jealous nerve that someone else is having the fun that only you should be having? Is it anger that your person "disobeyed" you, or a disappointment that your person suddenly isn't depending on you for that kind of enjoyment? Is sex the finish line that people in relationships have been looking forward to, and an outsider beating you there is just too embarrassing? I think it's the exclusiveness of sex that makes people feel uncomfortable when cheating happens. Anyone can see your person, anyone can talk to your person, anyone can hear your person. Those are all things that happen in public. But to be able to have sex, you have to have special access and permission. It's not something that anyone and everyone can do without permission. When cheating happens, the cheater has reduced their special person to just another person. The one who got cheated on doesn't feel like the winner or the V.I.P. anymore, they just feel miscellaneous.
- Suppose that sex is some kind of physical celebration between two people who want to express themselves to each other in that way. If you're cheating and having celebratory sex with the relationship outsider, what are you celebrating? The fact that you and this relationship outsider are getting away with something? The fact that you are not being a good friend to the person you're in a relationship with? The fact that you are not worth being friends with?
-

QUESTIONS TO GET ANSWERS TO

Don't ask these questions as if it's an interview. That's boring. Just try to learn these things about the person whether you ask curiously, listen, meditate, pray, observe...

In other words, STUDY the person!

Before you read this section, remember, though these questions are not commonly asked, YOU NEED TO KNOW the answers! BE BRAVE!!!!!!!!!!!

Oh, and don't be sarcastic or authoritative. This is just a way to collect facts, fill in the blanks in your mind and then see how you feel about them. Most people end up whining and complaining because they never knew the answers to these kinds of questions.

People's willingness and comfort level to answer certain questions tells a lot about them. It could be bad, good or just something to keep in mind. Disclaimer: just because someone is uncomfortable, unready or unsure about answering these questions doesn't mean they're guilty of anything. It just means that it is a potent question to that person.

(Some questions overlap or are similar, just to have a good dragnet to catch "everything".)

- How easily are you convinced, persuaded, influenced?
- How much self-control do you have?

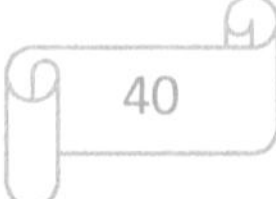

- How much self-control do you/will you have when I'm not with you?
- Do you have any unfinished business with anyone?
- Do you have any leftover feelings for anyone?
- Do you still feel like flirting with anyone?
- Do you daydream about anyone?
- What are your habits and hobbies?
- Do you think we'll get along?

- How long do you think we'll get along?
- How is your life going to affect my life?
- How much do you think you'll keep in contact with me, in what ways?
- How hard or easy will it be for me to talk to you about stuff that makes you uncomfortable?
- How much do you want/need me to keep in contact with you? In what ways?
- How well do you know the person and how well does the person know him/herself?
- Is there anyone else you had hopes on?
- Are you available to anyone else in any way? (Sex, dates, cuddling, flirting, emotional emergencies?)
- What would make you suffer in a relationship?
- Are you suffering from anything in any way?
- What makes you mad?
- What would make you so mad you'd want to hit me?
- What would make you so mad you'd want to leave me?
- What would make you so mad you'd want to be mean to me?
- How do you handle stress? With patience, violence, ignore it? Other?

- How do you feel about money?
- How much time and attention can you give me?
- ***What's going to be the difference between you now and you after I get to know you?***
- What's the best case scenario for our relationship?
- What's the worst case scenario for our relationship?
- What could I do that would anger you, bore you, embarrass you? Etc.
- Are you mean? How mean are you?
- Do you act different around different people?
- Do you have any flirt partners?
- What's your mental pace?
- What's your social rhythm?
- Do you still have hope for any relationships out there?
- Are you still trying to get over anyone?
- How will you know if/when you're ready for a relationship?
- How will I know if/when you're ready for a relationship?
- Any physical, social or emotional momentum with anyone else?

- What are your weaknesses in relationships?
- What do people love and hate about you?
- Do you have a crush on anyone, attracted to anyone?
- What's your lifestyle like?
    - Are you a stationary person? A homebody?
    - Are you active, lively, an out-and-about person?
- Is your person convinced about you or are you just a convenience to that person?
- Are you of importance to your person, or are you just considered a convenience?
- Any wild cards that could make a comeback?

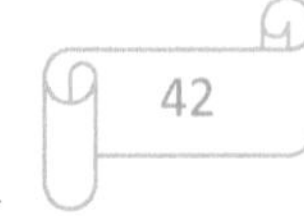

- What should we do if we get in to a fight or get mad at each other?
- Do you have any warrants?
- What would your friends tell me about you?
- What is important to you?
- Is this person suicidal?
  - If so, it could either be a situation in which you should be sympathetic, supportive and be a hero or it could be a situation in which you should be alarmed and out of the way.
  - It could be that the person is just having a hard time in life and needs an outlet, or it could be that the person is serious about hurting himself/herself and others.
- What do you expect to experience in life?
- What makes you happy?
- What gets on your nerves?
- Do you have any enemies?
- HOW IS YOUR HEALTH?
- How will your friends feel about me?
- Tell me about your temper.
- Does your person keep up with current events, environmental issues, health Issues, humanitarian issues, etc.? Do you care?
- What kind of experiences have you been exposed to?
- Do you have any secrets that would interrupt or interfere with our relationship if/when I find out?
- What would your ex do or say if we see him/her in public?
- Are you on call/on standby for anyone?
- Define FUN!!!!
- What's your reputation?
- Is the person fighting any mental battles right now?
  - Can the person handle them?

- How is the person handling them?
- Don't assume that a person fighting a mental battle is "crazy" and useless.
- Many people fighting mental battles are just that, FIGHTERS!, and they are worth knowing. You might be impressed by their daily fight to win their lives back from the problem or condition.
- Mental battles, in this context, could mean mental disorders, severe problems in life that they are struggling to solve, etc.

- How would your last boyfriend/girlfriend describe you?
- What kind of trouble would you possibly get me in to?
- Do you have goals for your mind, body and soul? What are they?
- What's the best and worst thing that ever happened to you?
- Do you have any secret habits?
- Are you single? Would anyone disagree?
- What are your views of marriage?
- What are your chances of cheating?
- Who else has your attention?
- Do you have a crush on anyone? (Its natural and it wouldn't be a surprise if the person you like didn't have a crush on ANYONE. Just find out how much momentum is behind the crush, if there is one.)
- Are you a liar?
- How will you treat me?
- Do people trust you?
- Do you care about people's feelings?
- Are you wild or mild?
- How do you feel about domestic violence against men? Against women?
- If I don't feel safe around you, what should I do?

- What's the worst thing you would do to me if you were mad (at me)?
- How hard or easy is it for you to handle things that are not going your way?
- How do you treat people who make you unhappy?
- What's your person's comfort level with temperatures, noise levels, etc...? Those things end up mattering the more you are involved in each other's environments.
- What do you think is the best and worst part of a relationship?
- What would you do if you felt jealous?
- What would you do if I was in danger?
- What would you do if we were in danger?
- What you do if you were in danger?
- What do you mean by "I'm working on myself"?
  - Is the person an addict? A thief? A bully?
  - What exactly is the person working on?
  - I've heard (about) women saying this a lot. Sometimes it's an excuse, sometimes it's legit, sometimes it's an exaggeration.
  - Is it something you can help the person with?
  - How long has the person been working on himself/herself?
  - Is it something serious?
  - Is it something you want to be bothered with?
  - Is the person overreacting?

SUGGESTIONS

- Marriage huddle vs. Marriage counseling.
  - Have a marriage huddle before you get married. Counseling has a bad connotation to it. It implies something is wrong. Why get married if something is wrong with the relationship? Also, a marriage counselor should not be telling the bride and groom how to problem solve or help them get to know each other. That is what dating is for. Fiancés should have already been through full cycles of feelings, emotions, moods, attitudes and all that before they get married. They should get married because they know each other and are satisfied with each other, not because they are looking forward to getting to know each other. A marriage huddle is similar to what a team does before a game. Since the team has already practiced and has already thought through the best and worst case scenarios, they can huddle up and motivate each other when the time comes.
  - **HOPEFULLY** the bride and groom can have a huddle, because they're ready for marriage, rather than have pre-marital counseling.
  - It should be like a pep rally vs. devil's advocate meeting. The relationship members should've played devil's advocate with each other about the relationship long before getting married.
- Let the person be human.

  - How dare you not let your person do human things like be mad, unsatisfied, share, sad, etc.?

  - Your person shouldn't stay that way, especially if you love the person, you'll want to help them improve their mood.

- But, they should have the same freedom of moods that yourself and everyone else has in life.
- How can you not let the person be human, especially if you love the person?

- Problem solving vs. person solving. People are busy trying to solve the person instead of the problem.
  - If there is a problem in your relationship, the problem should be center of attention not the people. Be mad at the problem, not at each other. Attack the problem, not each other. The problem is the enemy. Solve the problem; don't try to solve each other.
- Problems should be solved, not saved.
  - Don't let a problem go on just so there's something to pay attention to.
  - Pay attention to each other instead.
  - Preserve the relationship, not the problem.
- If you can't think out loud the way you think to yourself, you are not with the right person, or you need to establish a new comfort level.
- Participate in your person's life, don't dominate it.
- Don't loiter in relationships.
- DON'T SETTLE FOR SOMEONE you're not satisfied with. You'll regret it.
- Don't skip steps.
- More complaints than compliments about your relationship or person? Fix them or exit the relationship.
- Conduct yourself as if your person is always with you
- Don't babysit each other in a relationship. If you have to babysit each other, you shouldn't be together. If you are uncomfortable to the point that you can't concentrate because you don't trust the person, get over it or get out of it (the relationship).
- Assess instead of assume

  - Figure out what's really happening, what's really bothering you, what's really possible vs. impossible when it comes to any suspicions or concerns.
- Shape vs. escape
  - Don't try to escape uncomfortable situations, conversations, fights, etc. Try to shape them, together, shape them in to more comfortable situations.
- Share and volunteer information. If you don't want to, you shouldn't be in that relationship.
- Feelings are not miscellaneous so **express, explore, explain, examine, and exchange feelings.**
- Give because you want to, not because you want something.
  - You're not being fair or honest if you're giving your time, attention, gifts, anything....if you're doing because you expect sex, a relationship, money, favors, credit, etc. in return. You're supposed to give because you want your person to have whatever you're giving, NOT because you want something back. You're setting yourself up for frustration if you give because you want something back. Give because you want them to have whatever it is you're giving.
- Make small talk about the people in your daily life so your person isn't surprised or confused if/when you mention those people later.
- Anti-social media
  - Don't give the social media (internet) world, the same attention, time or experiences that you should only be giving to your person.
  - Be mindful of the thoughts, feelings, images and videos you are sharing. You are not in a relationship with the world and so the world is not equal to your person. Therefore, the world

does not deserve all of the same information, experiences and access to you that your person has.

- DON'T attract trouble to your relationship.
- There's no privacy in a marriage, no secrecy.
    - Your spouse is not your tag-a-long with limited access to you or your life. Your spouse is your love-twin.
- In dating, there's no secrecy, but some privacy is ok.
    - Your boyfriend/girlfriend is still a stranger in many ways. But...
    - Your (potential) boyfriend/girlfriend deserves for you to be up front about anything that will affect their life, health, feelings, reputation, safety, etc.
- If you don't trust your person, justify it.
    - Address and discuss it.
- Become mentally intimate with your person.
    - Get detailed.
- Be with who's best for you.
- Don't commute old relationship habits, expectations, etc. to your new relationship.
    - It's not fair to yourself or your person to expect them to recreate aspects of your old relationship. If you do, you're not letting your person be himself/herself. Also, if you're trying to recreate your old relationship, you should have stayed in it.
    - If your new relationship reflects your old one in some satisfactory ways, good for you, but those things should develop and not be scheduled. That way your relationship is fresh and new, not copied.
- SEX:
    - **Right person at the right time for the right reason**
    - Enjoy the events and moments of figuring each other out. It'll come naturally and/or eventually.

- THINK OUT LOUD together.
- Trust your instincts. If BOTH of you know you're in love or comfortable with each other, GO FOR IT! I'M A FAN OF YOURS ALREADY! But if you're not sure, then just don't be sure. It's simple.
- Don't settle for someone who won't let you be yourself. HOPEFULLY you were being yourself all the way up until the day you met that person. HOPEFULLY you were being yourself, using your own sense of humor, dressing how you like, talking how you like, and living how you like. If you can't be yourself, be careful of that relationship. Obviously if there are some changes you should make for the better, make them, if you feel like it. If not, leave each other alone. -
- Don't assume that because you had sex with someone that the person is going to care. Some people just enjoy sex with you and not take it seriously. It might not be meaningful or important to that person to have sex with you. Based on social chatter, sex to some people is just fun, just recreational, just something to do, just an activity. If you KNOW sex means a lot to you and trading your body for a relationship or love or something is important, say it. Say it and stick to it.
- Don't settle for less than you deserve, DESERVE being the key word.
- If you're in a bad relationship, either fix it or forget it.
- Don't use people or waste their time. Don't use them for sex, for money, for anything. Using someone means you are dependent on him/her. Don't use them for company either. I always tell people to be with whom they BELONG with. Don't use anyone because if you don't really want them, then they BELONG with someone else. Set them free and set yourself free. It might be a

little boring in the meantime, but find a way to use your time. Go get in shape if you're not already in shape. Go learn something. Go help someone. Stop wasting people's time, including your own. If you decide to spend any kind of time or energy on a person, then enJ☺Y that time. If it's going to be long term, it will be obvious eventually.

- Don't settle for someone whom you're embarrassed to be with. Yeah yeah yeah, everybody is somebody and all that goody goodness, but bottom line, if you're not comfortable with someone because of how they look, sound, talk, walk, whatever....do both of yourselves a favor and leave each other alone.
- Speaking of which, the guilt and shame tricks are so weak. Don't try to guilt someone in to being with you. If someone wants to be with you, they'll make it obvious. Even the shyest of people find their ways to make things obvious. Why would you want to be with someone who doesn't really want you, but is with you because you made them feel guilty?
- Don't lie to yourself just because you don't want to be alone. You already know good and well if the other person is too fat, too skinny, too ugly, too popular for your comfort level, too materialistic, too serious, too mean, too this, too that. YOU ALREADY KNOW! Why are you wasting your time trying to pretend like you're enjoying yourself when you're not? You already know that person isn't in to you like that. You already know that person is not your type. You already know. Just set yourself and the other person free.

- Take criticism seriously like people do with teachers, managers and coaches.

- People understand when these kinds of people tell us what we need to do better, but somehow people don't like it when the person who really needs to be impressed tells them the same thing. People maybe want to feel like they are already perfect in the eyes of their person. Maybe people assume that their partners think they are perfect and can't handle the shock that their partner has a complaint. Even so, how can you take (constructive) criticism from teachers, managers and coaches, in order to impress and satisfy them, but not your loved one?!!?!

- Be able to take a joke.
  -Don't lose your sense of humor and get sensitive if that you're in a relationship or on the verge of one.
- Don't be too shy to ask if your person is diseased in any way. Both of you will be affecting each other's health. This is not just pertaining to sexual health. I mean hygiene and how clean or filthy a person's home is, etc.
- Introduce your concerns with suffering language instead of angry language. EXAMPLE:
  - "I don't' trust you" vs. "I'm having trouble trusting you". If you don't trust the person, get out of the relationship. But if you intend to stay in it, saying something like "I'm having trouble trusting you" makes it obvious that you want to fix that problem. When you simply say "I don't trust you", there's no space for a response or for further discussion. It's just a statement without a stage.
  - I'm not confident in this relationship right now.
  - This relationship hasn't been fun for me lately.
  - All of the language in these examples gets attention, even if it doesn't get a reaction right away. But, it sets a stage for your person to step on and participate.
- Don't try to prevent the special event of love. Don't miss out.
- Don't be accusatory, be accurate.

- Don't overreact.
- Don't expect a non-human reaction to everything.
  - People have the capacity to cry, pout, be angry, etc.
  - Don't be surprised if your person does some of these HUMAN things sometimes.
- Don't assign feelings, personalities, answers, decisions, etc...
  - Don't tell your person how they do or don't feel. That's like telling someone else how hungry they are. You may have an IDEA, but more than likely, you don't know.
- Don't let outsiders, including me, design or redesign YOUR relationship. That's between the people in the relationship. This book is just giving you some ideas on what to think about when you're designing it. But you do what's best for you.
- Don't be sarcastic, be FANTASTIC!
- Don't do things that are going to backfire on you.
- Allow time to finish a feeling, a mood.
  - Again, people are human. Have enough courtesy to let people finish their moods so they don't sneak back up on them later.
  - Of course you don't want your person crying, pouting, feeling down, BUT those feelings came up for a reason. Let the person finish studying those feelings and solving those problems.
  - Interrupting someone who is resolving an issue thoroughly just results in the problem lingering.
  - Interrupting those moments for your own selfish reasons is rude. Remember, if you have a good friendship with your person, then do for them what you would do for any good friend, be there for them. It's not your show at that moment. Be on standby. Be available.
  - Don't distract the person from examining those feelings and trying to make sense of things. Don't try to change the subject, that's counterproductive.
  - I'm not saying to loiter on the subject, but figure it out. We have feelings for reasons. Feelings are not defects. Feelings are a part of our survival kits.
- Get mentally intimate.

   - You should understand each other's thought processes and reasoning.
- Enemy in your home
   - Home is the place where you should be able to relax and let your guard down. If your person lives with you, or visits a lot, and you can't let your mental, physical, emotional and overall guards down because of the other person, address it and problem solve, or excuse yourself from the relationship.
- If necessary, consider redoing your relationship, instead of undoing it.

Suggestions for men

- If your relationship isn't working out, or especially if she wants to be through with you, give it your best, try to win her back, but then let her be comfortable and do what she wants to do. She's not "yours". She chose to be involved with you, and at some point, chose to STOP being involved with you. Don't kill the women, rob them, threaten them, beat them up, humiliate them or ruin their lives. Those aren't the right things to do. Also, you're wasting time if you do the wrong things, time that you could be spending with the right woman. If things don't work out, pout if you have to, miss them if you have to, then change the subject. Even if you get unhappy, bounce back and keep it moving.

- Don't be a gatekeeper. Don't think you're the only man on the planet. Your woman had friends and family long before she met you unless you grew up together. She has friends from schools, her old town, her jobs, her sister's friends, her brother's friends...

Don't be foolish, selfish, or childish and restrict her from socializing/communicating. If you don't trust her, don't be with her. Don't harass her, DON'T HOLD HER HOSTAGE; don't threaten her or her male friends. Grow up and have a talk with her.

- Don't "defend" your woman if she's not in danger. Just because someone's speaking with her, it doesn't mean she's UNDER ATTACK!
  - Don't overreact.

  - I'm not saying you have to wait your turn to get your woman's attention or forfeit your manhood, but don't overreact just because she's socializing. Again, if you're friends with her, which you should be, do what you would do if any of your regular female friends were socializing with someone: get involved as necessary.

- Remember, there's a 50/50 chance you're going to get a woman pregnant if you're having sex. You're either going to impregnate her or you're not. No matter what contraceptives you're using and what promises or guarantees are made on behalf of the product. Point being, don't blame yourself or the woman if you impregnate her and suddenly the mood of your relationship changes because you and this semi-friend are going to become parents. If you blame anything, "blame" nature.

- Men are supposed to be productive and protective by nature. Wasting time with the wrong women means you're going to be off schedule with making your own woman happy. You'll be late. How can you protect the love of your life if you're not even present in her life? Who's protecting her? Who's in her life in the meantime? Who's making an impression on her while you're trying to make an impression on everyone else?

- If you have children with different women and are considered to be a seasonal or an occasional parent, realize that you are being thought of as a man who didn't finish what he started.

    - You started a family, or families, and didn't finish them. Any new woman you meet is going to view you as a man who can't finish what he starts, or as a man who won't finish what he starts. She's automatically going to be uncomfortable, even if she doesn't make it obvious to you.

    - (There's a difference between being a part-time parent and a full-time parent who doesn't see their children don't live in their household. Part-time parents/Dads are not as active or present in their children's lives as they should be. Full time parents/Dads whose children live with their mothers are men who basically do everything except tuck their children in every night.)
    - Your level of involvement, follow up, consistency, availability and interest in your children's lives will make a difference in how serious she takes you.

Suggestions for women

- Don't think because you impress a man sexually that he's going to concentrate on you. There's more to a relationship than sex. Sex, no matter how good it is, is only so impressive. People have needs

beyond sex. People need to be able to talk to someone, even when they don't feel like it. People need to be able to trust and depend on someone. People need to be able to get to the point with someone without worrying about hurting feelings. People don't want to tiptoe when they're talking all the time. As people, and I mean both men and women, we have to be able to be comfortable with a person. We all want to be able to be supported in different ways and to know that someone is in our corner, on our side. Sex is not the answer to that. Who cares if you can impress a man sexually if he doesn't like your personality? Who cares about your sex if he calls someone else to talk when he needs to? Who cares about your sex when he would rather go on a date with someone else? Get the point? If not, you're going to have bad luck.

- Don't try too hard! You're a woman. Relax. Men want you. Men even want "ugly" girls just because they're girls. Why are you trying so hard? Don't overdo the makeup, don't have all the surgeries as bait for mates (mate-bait), don't overthink your wardrobe. BE YOURSELF! Don't go out of your way. Don't try to buy him. Don't try to satisfy him. Just be yourself. Let him see who YOU are.

- If you are a single Mother, try saying "I am a Mother of (# of children)" instead of saying "I have (#) kids."

  - In my opinion, when you say you "have" something, it makes people think of everything that comes along with having it, how you got it, and it drums up several follow up questions that all end up distracting from you.

- When you say you have a car, it makes people want to talk about the car. When you say you have a dog or a job, it makes people want to talk about those things.
- BUT, if you say "I AM a Mother of (#) children" that makes the listener want to talk about you! That sounds so much more impressive than "I have (#) kids."
- We all know what Mothers are, who they are, and who they are supposed to be. We know the roles they play in people's lives. When you say you are a "***Mother*** of (number of children)", you have just given yourself a *title*, instead of an inventory!

- Remember, there's a 50/50 chance you're going to get pregnant if you're having sex. You're either going to get pregnant or you're not. No matter what contraceptives you're using and what promises or guarantees are made on behalf of the product. Point being, don't blame yourself or the guy if you get pregnant and suddenly the mood of your relationship changes because you and this semi-friend are going to become parents. If you blame anything, "blame" nature.

LASTLY

My fiancee wanted me to leave this part (below) in, I wrote it in the draft version of this book, when it was in a journal format. I was getting ready to go out of town to my friend's wedding.

"Anyway, I miss my friend, she's cool. She's like my heart. I miss her and I'm still here in Chicago."

This book is only meant to be a conversation starter. I hope this content leads to social changes, discussions, better relationships, happiness and all that special stuff!

Ok, the end.

P.S. – This is a love pyramid I made loooooong ago. Just wanted to share it. Just something I thought of one day. Thanks for reading my booooook!

Eddie L. Rogers II

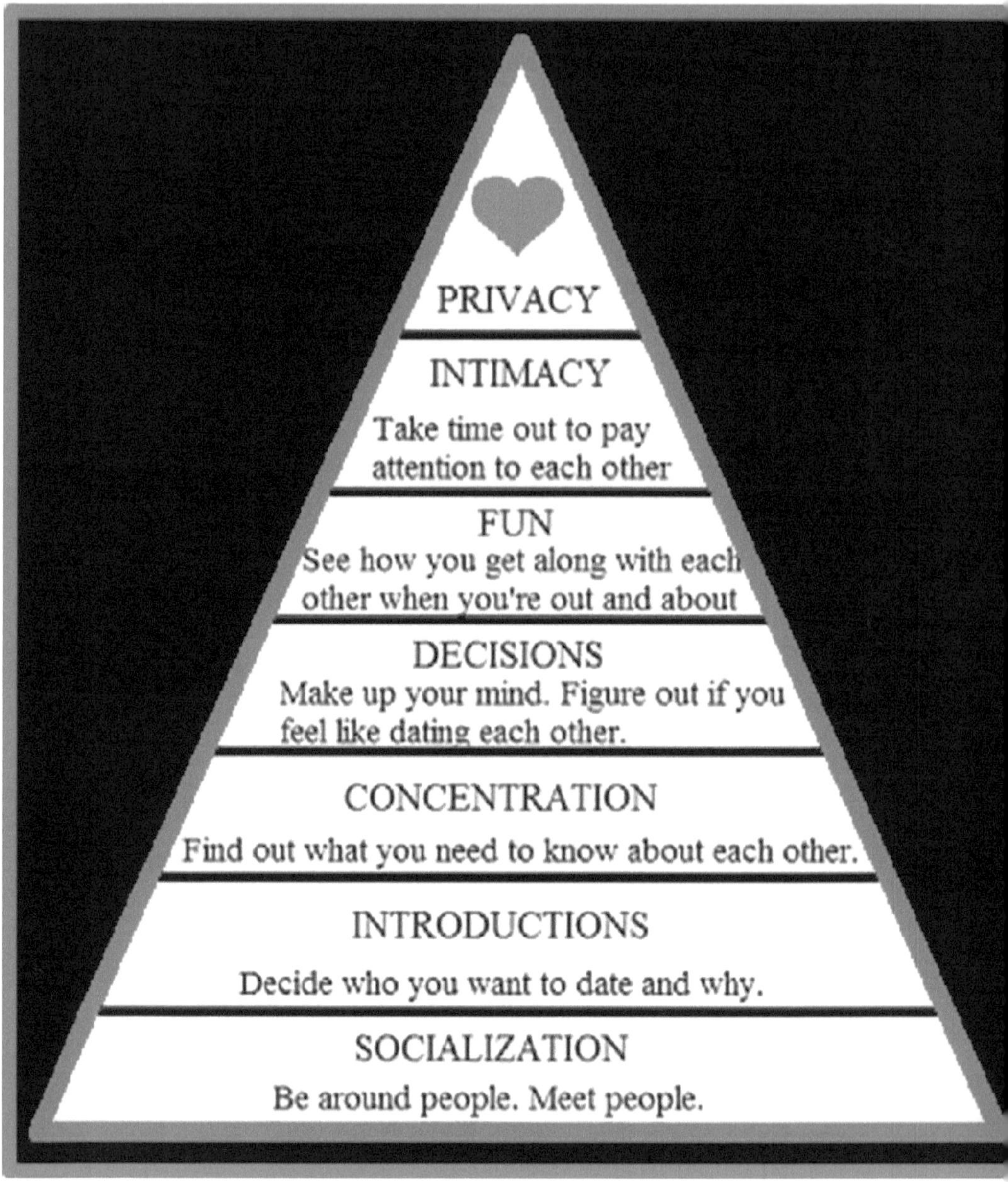

PRIVACY

INTIMACY

Take time out to pay attention to each other

FUN

See how you get along with each other when you're out and about

DECISIONS

Make up your mind. Figure out if you feel like dating each other.

CONCENTRATION

Find out what you need to know about each other.

INTRODUCTIONS

Decide who you want to date and why.

SOCIALIZATION

Be around people. Meet people.

About the Author:

I am Eddie L. Rogers II, the founder of www.Creaternity.org

Creaternity is the outlet I created for all of my creative endeavors including arts, music, literature, inventions, facilities and various service-oriented businesses.

I have a BA in Psychology and a BA in Mathematics.

This book is the accumulation of my observations, thoughts, experiences and feelings about relationships.

Some other upcoming books and *essays* by the author:

- The God Odyssey
- Psyche Decay
- Sexterior
- Your Career Hero
- CHOICES & CHANCES
- Infinity, Unfinity, Nonfinity
- Math, in other words
- The Trouble with the Truth
- CHAMPion vs. CHUMPion
- LIFE FLUENCY
- The Five Facts
- *Ghettomania*
- *Truicidal*
- *Naturalicious*

And more...

Createrinity's Homemade Music Division will be releasing

- 'SEVERELY IN LOVE' from the album LISTEN FOR THE LESSON!
- The vocal album 'For the Love of Love'
- **And more…**

www.ingramcontent.com/pod-product-compliance
Ingram Content Group UK Ltd.
Pitfield, Milton Keynes, MK11 3LW, UK
UKHW041915190726
13854UKWH00003B/1254